The Book of Whispers

☆ ☆ ☆ ☆ ☆ ☆ ☆ ☆ ☆ ☆ ☆ * ☆ ☆ ☆

Julie O'Callaghan

faber and faber

First published in 2006
by Faber and Faber Limited
3 Queen Square London WC1N 3AU

Published in the United States by Faber and Faber Inc.
an affiliate of Farrar, Straus and Giroux LLC, New York.

Typeset by Faber and Faber Limited
Printed in England by Mackays of Chatham plc, Chatham, Kent
All rights reserved

A CIP record for this book
is available from the British Library

ISBN 0–571–22768–6

☆

10 9 8 7 6 5 4 3 2 1

Contents

The Book of Whispers

Warning!

Do not attempt
to speak these poems
in a 'normal' tone
of voice. Failure to
whisper them
may result in permanent
poem damage.

☆ ☆ ☆ ☆ ☆ ☆ ☆ ☆ ☆ * ☆ ☆ ☆

Let's Stop Shouting – Shall We????

I'm not sure
you want to face these
difficult facts
but here goes:
everyone is
hollering
screaming
shouting
yelling.
Rappers
ads on TV
politicians on the news
fanatics
teachers
parents.
Listen up campers
whispering is the
way forward.
Whispering is
essential.
Whispering is the
buzz
of the future.
So why not just give in
and get with the programme:

WHISPER.

Tips for Whisperers

always aim whisper
at person's ear

roll paper into cone
speak at narrow end

if whispering on phone
hide in closet

roll hand into tunnel
speak at either end

don't hide behind book
when in class

don't whisper loudly
if saying nasty stuff

don't whisper nasty stuff
gives whispering bad name

whisper
when whispered to

don't keep saying
what

☆ ☆ ☆ ☆ ☆ ☆ ☆ ☆ ☆ ☆ ☆ ✱ ☆ ☆ ☆

Good Advice

A voice in my head is whispering good advice.
Such as, *Don't eat that candy bar, you'll regret it*
or, *Maybe you ought to go and help your mom*
or, *How about some study? – there's a test tomorrow.*
I have no idea how
a whisperer came into my head
suggesting what I should do.
It whispers to me every day
and seems to wake at the same time as me.
Some kids think I'm nuts
to take orders from a munchkin
I never met.
But then I hear a whisper:
Don't listen to a word they say.

☆ ☆ ☆ ☆ ☆ ☆ ☆ ☆ ☆ ☆ * ☆ ☆ ☆

Whispering in History

I know that Emily told you
that Sarah was invited to
Ruth's birthday party on Saturday.
But she was only eavesdropping
on Catherine and Lizzie
in the changing room after gym
and when Emily *thought*
she heard the name Sarah
it was *really* Mary.
So will you come to the party?
Ruth told me that she was having
a make-up expert showing
how to do lipstick and eyeliner
and the cake is made out of
chocolate ice cream and marshmallows.
Yes Miss Miller – I'm listening.
So what time will my mom
pick you up?

☆ ☆ ☆ ☆ ☆ ☆ ☆ ☆ ☆ ☆ * ☆ ☆ ☆

No Talking

Ladies, would you please lower
your voices?
The other readers
are trying to concentrate.
If you urgently need to discuss
the price of various
belly tops I must ask you
to kindly do so
outside.

Wildlife Whispers

If you want to observe the wildlife
in my garden, then whispering
is real important.
I learned that off the TV.
Like how the chameleon sitting
on the lily-of-the-valley there
would scurry away
if you started screaming
with excitement.
When I lift this sheet
from the clothesline,
the family of baby hedgehogs
are happier when you whisper:
their ears are so teensy
loud noises gives them a headache.
The wren clinging to the trellis
would fly off and hide in a bush
if you weren't whispering.
That goes for the robin
and the blackbird too.
Bunnies, kittens – you name it –
don't all love loud voices,
so take it from me:
whisper around animals
and you can't go wrong.

Earth Whispers

White

when rain
whispers
it is snow

Green

when leaves
whisper
it is spring

Blue

when sky
whispers
it is wind

Grey

when cloud
whispers
it is wet

Red

when day
whispers
it is dusk

Purple

when hills
whisper
it is far

Yellow

when sun
whispers
it is heat

Black

when night
whispers
it is sleep

☆ ☆ ☆ ☆ ☆ ☆ ☆ ☆ ☆ ☆ * ☆ ☆ ☆

Surprise

Do you think you could
stop poking your knee
into my back?
It's rotten enough crouching
under a dining-room table
in the dark
waiting for the birthday girl to arrive
for her surprise party
without ruining my back too.
I'm not a fan of surprise parties.
If I hadn't seen the Devil's Food layer cake
out in the kitchen
I might have just gone
home before we all
started acting like idiots
looking for places to hide.
Feet are coming
up the porch steps.
I guess I'll pretend
to be enthusiastic
when we all scream
the S-word.

Prayer

Dear Lord,
if only you will let me
have an iPod
I won't ever swear again.
I'll tell my mom
to put up her feet
and allow me to do the dishes
and I will only use it after
I've done my homework
and besides that
it is quite educational
so it might help my grades somewhat
and also it is on special offer
so my parents won't have
to fork out that much money either.
Amen.

☆ ☆ ☆ ☆ ☆ ☆ ☆ ☆ ☆ * ☆ ☆

Another Prayer

Dear God,
if you make this zit disappear
I will only eat french fries
on rare occasions
like getting a good report card
or winning a basketball game.
Does that sound fair?
It's a small zit, I admit,
but why o why
did you have to
put it on my nose?
That wasn't very Christian
now was it?

Before the Recital

I never thought I would be standing here
on the side of a dark stage
dressed in a gorgeous outfit
waiting to play the piano.
I'm very nervous.
I peeked out and saw
the rows and rows
of people all staring up.
You sit in the spotlight
and hit the keys.
Some woman said I'm
on in five minutes
so I will breathe deeply
and try to stay calm.
I hope I can make it
to the piano bench
without tripping.
Wish me luck.

☆ ☆ ☆ ☆ ☆ ☆ ☆ ☆ ☆ ☆ ☆ ✦ ☆ ☆ ☆

𝒲

who wouldn't whisper
wow – why
when worried
when wondering
when wistful
when wishing
whispering works

without whispering –
what?

Whispering Leaves

I am wondering
what it is
the leaves are whispering to me.
Which language they speak.
It doesn't seem funny
but it might be.
It takes years
getting leaf ears
only there aren't
many quiet days
to sit out and learn
leaf talk.
Leaves, I'm listening.

Whispering in Church

Even little tiny babies realise
how it's a definite no-no
to talk and laugh
and horse around in church.
But there are a few exceptions
to the talking part.
Sometimes an emergency comes up –
like for instance if
the lady next to you
has her elbow in your ribs.
So I said to my sister,
'Move over, *somebody's*
hogging all the space.'
That was when Father Egan
roared down from the altar,
'The girl with the red hair-band
will leave this church –
NOW!'
Oh man – I had to walk
down the main aisle
with my red face and hair-band
feeling like a sinner.
I bet God will forgive me
for thinking Father Egan
is a stinker.

☆ ☆ ☆ ☆ ☆ ☆ ☆ ☆ ☆ ☆ * ☆ ☆

Mother-Daughter

Mom, please don't sit there.
What did you say, honey?
I said don't sit there.
Sweetie, why are you whispering?
I am trying to tell you something.
What is wrong with you?
I don't want to sit there.
I can't hear you.
Mom – I am NOT sitting there.
For heaven's sake why not?
Because I know that person.
What?
That guy is in my class.
Oh how nice – will I move over?
I'm leaving.

Not Polite

It's not polite
to whisper to someone
when another person
is sitting there
beside you
because they will think
you are saying something
unkind about them
since let's face it –
if it was something
great, why whisper?
Got that?
(Mom and Dad,
this goes for you too.)

S-T-I-T-C-H-E-S

when you bang your head
off the school bell
in the playground
and you get in line
and the kids are going
EUUUEEEGGGHHH
when they look at you
and then you glance down
at your new winter boots
and a big plop of blood
cascades from your forehead
onto them
and your teacher brings you
into the Principal's office
and tries not to panic
(you can tell)
and calls your mom
and then whispers
s-t-i-t-c-h-e-s into the phone
just believe me
1) you can hear
2) you can spell

☆ ☆ ☆ ☆ ☆ ☆ ☆ ☆ ☆ ★ ☆ ☆ ☆

Movies

How come that guy
is groping around in the dark
when he is supposed to be looking
for the kidnapped detective
and he could just turn on the light?
The switch is right there on the wall beside him.
All he needs to do is flick it
and he could see
what's in front of his face.
Oh and *of course* the bad guy
has night-vision goggles
and is watching him stumble
and bash into things.
Turn the light on, buddy!

SHHHHHHHHHH.

☆ ☆ ☆ ☆ ☆ ☆ ☆ ☆ ☆ ☆ ☆ ✳ ☆ ☆ ☆

Who

who whispers
to me
and when I turn
no one

☆ ☆ ☆ ☆ ☆ ☆ ☆ ☆ ☆ * ☆ ☆ ☆

Unhappy Whispers

I whispered a lot
in my father's final weeks.
Some days are so terrible
you can't speak
in a normal tone about them.

You lose your voice
when sad things happen
and whispering fills
your mouth with words
you cannot bear to hear.

Sleep-Over

I am *not* kidding –
my mom
will freak if she sees
cookie crumbs
in this bed tomorrow.
And (*quit talking so loud*)
just because we are
under the blankets
doesn't mean she won't
hear you singing.
She has x-ray ears.
How many cookies are left?
Point the flashlight over here.
Quit kicking
and let me see!
Ugh-oh – turn it off – quick.

Football Whispers

My voice is gone.
I hollered too much
at the game
and now
all I can do is whisper.
It is quite relaxing
and doesn't hurt
your eardrum
or your aching head
or your voice box either.
People keep saying
'speak up'
but no can do.
Victory is ours.

Laryngitis

I am so happy:
no talking.
It is ideal.
No chatting to anyone
about anything.
Arguments are history.
No explaining
no discussing
no excuses.
All I need to do
all day long
is to whisper
'Yes please'
when my mother
asks me if
I could swallow some
Ben & Jerry's ice cream.

Don't Wake the Baby

That's all I ever hear –
Don't make so much noise
you'll wake the baby.
Our family used to laugh and sing
jump up and down
and stand on our heads
and scream out to the kitchen
for more popcorn
and giggle like lunatics
and turn up the stereo
and yell at each other
about which TV show to watch
and holler at the dog
to stop chewing toys
and make a racket
and bang on things
and cry out
Stop bothering me
to anybody who was bothering us.
Now we sit around whispering
at the tops of our voices.

This kid better grow up soon!

☆ ☆ ☆ ☆ ☆ ☆ ☆ ☆ ☆ ☆ * ☆ ☆

Nutmeg

I am following
the recipe carefully
tossing in the flour
whisking up the eggs
combining sugar with butter
sprinkling a dash of vanilla
coated in nonsense
up to my elbows

When I come
to the part
where it suggests
I fold in the merest
whisper of nutmeg
I'd love to add
a gigantic shout
of chocolate instead

Horse Whispering

ME:

If you behave I'll give you treats:
I have Polo mints and a carrot
an apple and a handful of oats.
So remember that during the lesson
and don't buck or swerve or shy.
Deal?

HORSE:

no yanking on mouth
no whacking with stick
no jabbing in ribs
no bouncing on back
no speaking human
deal

Whispering to Pickles

Pickles, my guinea pig,
you are the only person
in the entire universe
who is my friend.
All those ratty girls at school
told me my clothes don't match
and that my hair is a disaster area.
But when I come home from school
there you are smiling up at me
waiting for a piece of celery
to munch on
while you listen carefully
to everything I tell you.
You never laugh at my hair
or look me up and down
and shake your head.
Pickles, I wish you were a human
and we could ride bikes together
and go and get an ice cream bar.
I don't blame you
for being a squirt
but maybe if I kiss you
you will morph into
a boy who will protect me
from nasty girls.
Would that be a possibility?

☆ ☆ ☆ ☆ ☆ ☆ ☆ ☆ ☆ ☆ ☆ ☆ ☆ ☆ ☆

Secret Closet

It's me in my mom's secret closet.
The one with the hidden door
behind her everyday clothes.
I just pulled her white satin wedding shoe
out from under my butt.
I need to make myself comfortable.
We're in the middle of hide-and-seek
and I am pretty sure no one will find me.
So I have to be careful
in case they hear me.
You wouldn't believe
what a fantastic place
this is to disappear.
Can you see a shirt with one arm
waving up and down?
That's my approximate position.
Oh and that's where I'll be
when they give up
and I win.

☆ ☆ ☆ ☆ ☆ ☆ ☆ ☆ ☆ ☆ * ☆ ☆ ☆

Store Whispers

See that lady over there:
do you think this blouse
would fit her?
No – I can't *ask* her –
it's for her birthday!
I know she likes polka dots
and that green is her favourite
colour and that she loves
ruffles down the front
so it's perfect for her.
The only problem is the size:
sometimes she looks curvy
and sometimes she looks thin
so it's hard to know which size to get.
She can always exchange it if it's wrong –
can't she?

☆ ☆ ☆ ☆ ☆ ☆ ☆ ☆ ☆ ☆ * ☆ ☆ ☆

What's That?

Hey, Katie, wake up.
Did you hear that noise?
It sounded like somebody
opening the door downstairs.
No – I *mean* it.
I really heard it.
Shhhh – hear that?
You *didn't*?
It was like a footstep
in the hall.
For crying out loud -
you *must've* heard that?
See? I told you.
I knew this baseball bat
would come in handy some day.

Christmas Whispers

I had to be brave
tiptoeing downstairs
in the middle of
a dark winter's night.
I was trying to avoid
the creaky parts of the stairs
but it seemed to make
the noise even louder.
The giant quiet pine tree
in our stairwell saw me
up at her top branches
travelling downwards.
She was lonesome for her forest.
I just needed to check
one detail
under her green skirts
so I could get to sleep
and stop wondering so much.
Jill was there – with a bow around her neck,
dressed in some cool doll's clothes
and almost as tall as me.
My name was on her tag.
GREAT.
I touched her hair
and flew up the stairs to bed.

Important Whispering

Here we have various examples
of whispering which are highly
beneficial to the human race.
Telling your friend her blouse is open.
(Really ALL whispering to inform people
of embarrassing clothes or nose
or teeth situations is of great use.)
A teacher at the side of a stage
whispering a forgotten line.
Your sister whispering
a perfect excuse to miss
your snobbish cousin's party.
Reminding someone of the punch line
to a joke they can't recall.
That goes for classrooms
during spot quizzes also.
Warning everyone
the teacher is coming.
Whispering RELAX to yourself
at tense moments.
Whispering to your mom
that you don't want to babysit
for the brat next door.
As you may have guessed
whispering is one of my all-time

☆ ☆ ☆ ☆ ☆ ☆ ☆ ☆ ☆ ☆ * ☆ ☆ ☆

favourite forms of communication.
Where would we be
without it?

Spread the Word

Go forth and whisper!